Famous American

Spies

By Lou Ann Walker

CELEBRATION PRESS

Pearson Learning Group

Contents

What Makes a Good Spy?

Mystery, danger, and excitement are often a part of the world of secret agents. Spies may secretly watch people, force their way into places, or have to **disguise** the way they look, feel, and normally act. They do all of these things to find out secret information.

For thousands of years, governments have paid people to spy. These governments want to find out what other countries may be secretly planning or doing. So why do people become spies? Some do it for money. Other spies are **patriotic** and want to help their country.

Some people spy for a country that is not their own. They steal secrets from their own country because they believe their government is doing something wrong. Then they sell or give the information to another country. Some spies even act as **double agents**. An enemy thinks double agents are working for them when the agents are really working for their own country.

Actor Pierce Brosnan portraying the fictional spy James Bond

Never forget that spies are often in danger. Many spies have been jailed while trying to uncover secrets to save their countries. Some have even been killed.

In adventure stories and movies, spies are often popular and glamorous characters. You may have heard of movies featuring James Bond, one of the most famous fictional spies. What goes on in true-life spying, though, is not the made-up adventure of an action movie.

George Washington, "Spymaster"

When the American colonies were fighting for their independence from Great Britain in the Revolutionary War, both the British and the colonists used spies. George Washington himself became a spymaster. He used a famous group known as the Culper Spy Ring. The name came from code names used by two of its leaders, Robert Townsend and Abraham Woodhull.

A spy gave George Washington the information he needed to cross the Delaware River and attack the British in December 1776.

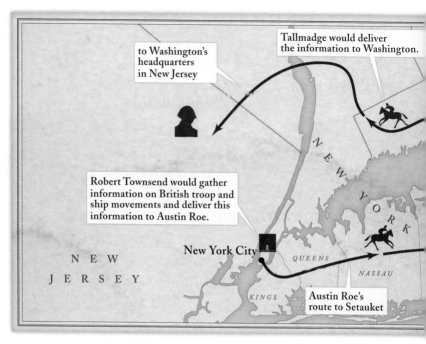

The route of the Culper Spy Ring

One plan was for "Samuel Culper Jr." (really Robert Townsend, a New York City shopkeeper and newspaper reporter) to gather information about British troop movements. A tavern owner, Austin Roe, visited Culper's store to collect the written information. Then Roe rode his horse to a farm in Setauket, Long Island, where he hid the documents. "Samuel Culper Sr." (whose real name was Abraham Woodhull) went to the farm to take the documents from a secret box.

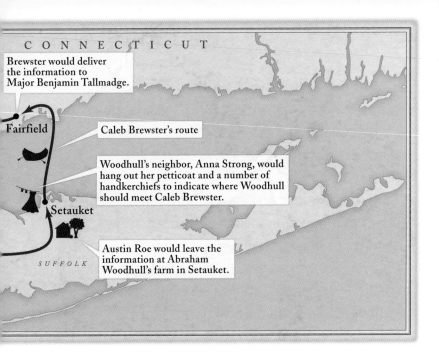

CONNECTICUT

Brewster would deliver the information to Major Benjamin Tallmadge.

Fairfield

Caleb Brewster's route

Woodhull's neighbor, Anna Strong, would hang out her petticoat and a number of handkerchiefs to indicate where Woodhull should meet Caleb Brewster.

Setauket

SUFFOLK

Austin Roe would leave the information at Abraham Woodhull's farm in Setauket.

Next, "Culper Sr." looked across the bay to see if a fellow spy, Anna Strong, had placed her black petticoat and some handkerchiefs on a clothesline. The petticoat meant that Caleb Brewster, another Culper spy, was waiting to row the documents across the bay. The number of handkerchiefs told which cove Brewster was hiding in. Brewster then rowed to Fairfield, Connecticut. He gave the documents to Major Benjamin Tallmadge, who went on to deliver them to George Washington.

After the British stole a letter from Washington meant for the Culper Spy Ring, Washington found new ways to keep their secrets safe. They began sending quill letters, which were messages hidden in feather quills from large birds. They used invisible ink and developed a secret code. Their codebook was like a dictionary in which each word had a number. For example, *Camp* was 73. *Enemy* was 178. The code was not cracked for nearly 150 years until Morton Pennypacker, a historian, figured it out.

George Washington didn't always have good luck with his spies. One of Washington's spies, Nathan Hale, was caught while on a mission trying to find out about British troop movements. After Hale was executed, one of his letters was found. It included a sentence that became one of the most famous statements in American history: "I only regret that I have but one life to lose for my country."

Nathan Hale showed great courage and loyalty to Washington and the colonists' cause. However, one of Washington's trusted generals, Benedict Arnold, became a traitor.

Information from the Culper Spy Ring probably helped capture Benedict Arnold, shown in this woodcut from 1780.

After being passed over for a promotion, General Arnold was angry. He decided to surrender an important fort he commanded at West Point to the British. Luckily, Arnold's plan was discovered before this fort on the Hudson River was lost. To this day, a traitor is often called a "Benedict Arnold."

As a spymaster, Washington was also an expert in spreading wrong information. After the war, a British man admitted, "Washington did not really outfight the British. He simply out-spied us."

Civil War Spies

During the Civil War, some of the best spies were women. Many women in the North (the Union) and in the South (the Confederacy) wanted to help their sides win. They also wanted to help their husbands and sons who were fighting in the war.

To help the war efforts, many women hid messages or weapons in their enormous hoop skirts and in their elaborately styled hair. While she was in prison, one spy even smuggled information out in other women's hair.

A famous Confederate female spy was good at sneaking into rooms to eavesdrop. She was arrested at least six times. One time, she persuaded the Northerner who caught her to marry her and switch to the Confederate side.

Sarah Emma Edmonds became a Union spy because she was deeply patriotic. She also liked adventure. Edmonds was living in Michigan when she heard that the Union needed soldiers.

Sarah Emma Edmonds disguised herself as many different people in order to spy for the Union Army.

DISGUISED AS A CONTRABAND.—Page 113.

Because women weren't allowed to become soldiers in the Civil War, Edmonds disguised herself as a man. She became Private Frank Thompson.

When Edmonds heard that the Union was looking for a spy, she volunteered. On her first mission, disguised as an African American slave, she learned the Confederates were painting logs black to make them look like cannons so the Union would think they had a lot of **artillery**.

About two months later, Edmonds dressed as an Irish peddler woman and sold goods in a Confederate camp. All the while she listened and watched to find out what she could. Once she had the information she needed, she took a horse and headed toward the Union camp. The Confederates followed, shooting at her and wounding her in the arm. She stayed in her saddle and returned safely to her camp.

When Edmonds developed malaria, she deserted and went to a hospital. She didn't want anyone in the army to find out she was a woman. After she recovered, she couldn't rejoin her army unit because Private Frank Thompson was listed as a deserter. So, she worked in Washington, D.C., as a nurse until the war ended.

Edmonds had 11 successful missions. "I am naturally fond of adventure," she said later in her life, "a little ambitious and a good deal romantic, but patriotism was the true secret of my success." In 1884, Congress gave Edmonds (alias Frank Thompson) an honorable discharge from the army, saying that "truth is oftentimes stranger than fiction."

During the Civil War, Harriet Tubman helped free many African American slaves.

Many Civil War spies were African American slaves who passed on information in hope that the North would win and slavery would be abolished throughout the United States. Harriet Tubman, a former slave herself, had already rescued hundreds of African Americans through the Underground Railroad before the Civil War began. This system of routes and safe homes was set up by people who helped slaves escape from the South to free states in the North and Canada.

Tubman was working as a nurse when, in 1863, she was asked by the Union Army to gather a network of African American men in South Carolina to act as spies. The men provided Tubman with important inside information. Soon, Tubman began leading spy missions herself.

She and Colonel James Montgomery of the Union Army were able to lead 150 African American soldiers on a Union gunboat raid of Confederates. Under the command of Colonel Montgomery, Tubman went on to lead troops who destroyed railroad lines and bridges in order to stop Confederate troops. She also freed slaves during these missions.

Despite her hard work, Tubman had to support herself by selling root beer, pies, and gingerbread. She was paid only $200 over three years for her help during the war. She must have been surprised when she saw posters offering a $40,000 reward for her capture. This was a huge amount of money for that time and proof of how useful she had been in her missions. Later, she was awarded a government **pension** for her service as a spy for the Union.

From Unimportant to Very Important

There was surprisingly little spying done during World War I. Many people in the U.S. government at that time felt spying wasn't dignified. When one U.S. government agency that was used to decode secret messages was closed in the 1920s, an official was said to have stated, "Gentlemen do not read each other's mail." Spies were not used much again until the 1940s.

A U.S. navy photographer readies his camera for a shot taken from an airplane in the early 1940s.

Moe Berg may have started his spying career while still playing professional baseball.

Soon after World War II began, however, gathering covert, or secret, information became very important to the United States in order to defeat Germany and Japan. President Franklin D. Roosevelt chose William J. Donovan to create the Office of Strategic Services (OSS).

One of the greatest spies of World War II was Moe Berg. He played professional baseball before deciding to become a spy. In 1943, after retiring from baseball, he joined the OSS.

Berg was born in a poor section of New York City. Charming and smart, he attended Princeton University, then went on to Columbia Law School. He was a secretive person. It was hard for others to get to know him. Many people who did know him thought that he enjoyed being mysterious and concluded that was the reason he became a spy.

Berg helped the OSS, which conducted spy operations overseas, in many ways. In 1944, Berg pretended to be a Swiss student in order to attend a lecture in Switzerland, given by Germany's top physicist. At the time, the U.S. government was afraid that Nazi Germany had learned how to create the atomic bomb. The United States knew if that were true, the Germans could win the war. The information Berg learned proved that Germany was not as far along as people had feared.

For another of his adventures, Berg traveled to Czechoslovakia, which was occupied by the Soviet Union. When Russian guards demanded that he show his **credentials**, Berg fooled them by holding up a letter with a large red star. The paper was really a letter from an oil company!

The famous singer Josephine Baker was also a spy during World War II. She had grown up poor in St. Louis, Missouri. By the time she was ten, she had quit school and was working to support her family.

As a teenager, Baker began dancing and moved to New York City to work on Broadway. In 1925, she moved to Paris and became one of the best-known entertainers in France. When the war broke out, Baker wanted to help the French forces working with the Allies (Great Britain, the Soviet Union, and the United States), the countries that had joined together to fight Germany. She had always been daring, and being a spy suited her well.

As Baker traveled around Europe entertaining troops, she collected information to send back to the Allies and the French forces. She pinned to her underwear notes and photos showing where Germany hid war equipment. Then she covered her dress with a big fur coat. Baker also carried sheet music on which secret information was written in invisible ink. The people to whom she delivered the music placed the sheets under a special light to view the information.

Josephine Baker pinned secret information and photos to her underwear in order to slip them past the enemy.

Even when Baker became sick and had to stay in bed for months, she remembered everything her visitors let slip about what the Nazis were doing in northern Africa. She then sent the information to the Allies. Baker's work was so important that, after the war, General Charles de Gaulle of France presented her with top military honors. When she died in 1975, Baker was given military honors at her funeral.

Spying Goes Super High-Tech

At the end of World War II, the OSS closed, but it had provided the basis for the Central Intelligence Agency (CIA), which was founded in 1947. The CIA is the federal government agency concerned with gathering intelligence and other activities that involve the nation's safety.

Spying was still important after the war because of the hostility that developed between the Soviet Union and the United States, an era known as the Cold War (1946–1991). After the Cold War, spying became an important tool against terrorism.

The U.S. government continues to develop high-level technology to help in the search for information. Military spy planes, such as the RB-47 from the 1960s, have often been used to gather information. Future spy planes may be robots as small as flying insects. Satellites and other electronic listening devices are increasingly used to replace much of the fieldwork that is done by agents.

Some people claim that Washington, D.C., has more working spies than any other city in the world. To satisfy the public's curiosity about spying, The International Spy Museum opened in Washington, D.C., in 2002.

At the museum, visitors can view **wire tapping** devices, buttonhole cameras, soda cans used to hide film, and an explosive that looks like a piece of coal. There are pens that shoot darts and rings that hide guns.

The International Spy Museum

Tools spies have used to perform their work include a shoe and a pen with radio transmitters and a wristwatch camera.

Museum visitors are encouraged to adopt a **cover**. At different points, the visitors are asked to give details about their covers. They can also test themselves on identifying common **surveillance** equipment and "dead drops" where spies would exchange money and information with others.

In other spots in the museum, visitors try to identify agents who are in disguise. They can also listen to conversations of other people in the museum captured by **bugs**.

Some of the more unusual objects in the museum's collection include the following:

- a 2,500-year-old book written by a Chinese military expert, promoting the use of spies
- a copy of a listening device disguised as a tree stump
- a radio that looks like a suitcase, used by Allied spies in World War II
- a bug that came with an explosive and a tiny parachute. Planted in a drain pipe, the bug would then eject into a sewer.

As people tour the museum, they learn about the lives of many famous spies. They read about the dangers of spying and how some well-known spies were caught. They also learn that many spies are never discovered. As one sign says, we discover the work of agents "only after they are captured, turn traitor, or come forward. The most successful spies will never be recognized, their missions never revealed." In the world of spying, secrecy is everything.

Glossary

artillery mounted guns that are too heavy to carry

bugs microphones hidden to record conversations secretly

cover a false identity that allows a person to pretend to be someone else

credentials proof that a person has the right to do something

disguise to hide a person's identity by changing the appearance

double agents spies employed by two countries

malaria a disease caused by the bite of a mosquito

patriotic loyal to and supportive of your country

pension regular payments of money paid to a person after retirement as a reward for service

spymaster the head of a ring of spies

surveillance keeping close watch over a person or group, usually without being spotted

wire tapping secretly listening to other people's conversations by connecting listening devices to their phones